Released on March 20, 2025

All pictures were taken and modified by Zineb Bizriken

All text was written by Zineb Bizriken

© Zineb Bizriken, 2025. All rights reserved.

Winterfall Ablaze Edition

Notes & Camera roll

Zineb Bizriken

To you who is now blooming

Quick intro/explanation

Notes & Camera Roll is a book series of poetry that will continue indefinitely. Every edition has a different name instead of a number to make sure everybody understands that order doesn't matter. For this series, the fourth edition can be read first without the need to read prior editions. You are free to join the ride whenever, turn back or continue from where you started.

From the title, you can see I called my poem notes. The reason is simply because that was their beginning. Not only were they written on a notes app, and or a notebook, but they were first a jotted down thought.

And as for 'Camera Roll', I wanted to colour my pages the best way I could. While I am not a good drawer, I'd say I enjoy taking pictures. And instead of letting my pictures rot away in my camera roll, why not utilize them to embellish my pages. All the photos I have taken, and modified to fit the poem's concept. That being said, I am a writer and photography is but a hobby that somehow ended up being helpful. The photos might not be of professional quality, but they did their job.

I'll let you read the book now. Enjoy :)

What you will find in this book:

Poems visualized with self-taken, self edited pictures

Pages of notes (poems that didn't make the cut/are unfinished and will probably remain unfinished)

A playlist with song recommendations

An option to submit your poetry for publication

A page where you can write your own poem!

Welcome

May my words wrap around your shoulders,
May they pat your back and lend you an ear,
May they accept your silence if that is your choice,
I trust they'll be free of judgment,
I trust they'll be unconditionally yours.

May you find kinship with my words,
May you hold them tight, for they'll never vanish first,
What you think of them shall be what they mean.

May they be the answer to your question
as well as the light you yearned for,
at night as you put yourself to sleep.

Zi.B

Untitled note

December 12, 2024   8:43 PM

Untitled notes crowd my phone,
which is also my creative space,
days are a muse and observations are without judgement.

I type anecdotes from unintentional eavesdropping,
my untitled notes hide no secret,
but they remain anonymous,
much like their lack of title,
the characters inside are nameless.

Untitled notes in my phone call on me to act,
to make use of words sourced from days I've lived.

-Zi.B

White night

I'm eating breakfast after a white night
cereals drowned in milk nearing expiration
the sun peeks out the neighbour's roof
my eyes are red, they beg for an end,
my mind forgoes their pleas and keeps on
for it finds comfort in vicious cycles
nostalgia bordering on familiarity
the past acts as a barricade
protecting me from the false enemy that is
my future.

Zi.B

POET NEWS

15TH OCTOBER — ZINEBBIZRIKEN.SPACE

FREAK

Source: Zineb Bizriken

People looked evil through your lens
I didn't care to reflect that in my world
you look for flaws while I notice them
you're a self-proclaimed fighter of justice
but apparently not everybody deserves that care
those bystanders are at fault in your eyes
and for what
I could never tell.

You're morbid and don't even realize it
the news is for you a source of entertainment
you're on fire and burn all that is near you
keep burning away
for all you'll be left with
are the ashes of what was.

Zi.B

The Daydream

The wavering promise of a
daydream,
fuelled by the fickle mind,
seldom makes it to the finish line,
for it's never received faith.

The daydream lingers with specks
of hope,
it longs to be remembered,
to be treasured and given trust,
for its strength surpasses that of
human senses.

Zi.B

Burns

You   Reached your hand   to the fire

you said: "what burns   finds its way   back,"

then   shafts of light   crossed your   path,

through the havoc,   you paved,

for you knew   glory   was likely,

had you chosen   to walk   past the fire,

you'd spend   a lifetime   a corpse.

Zi.B

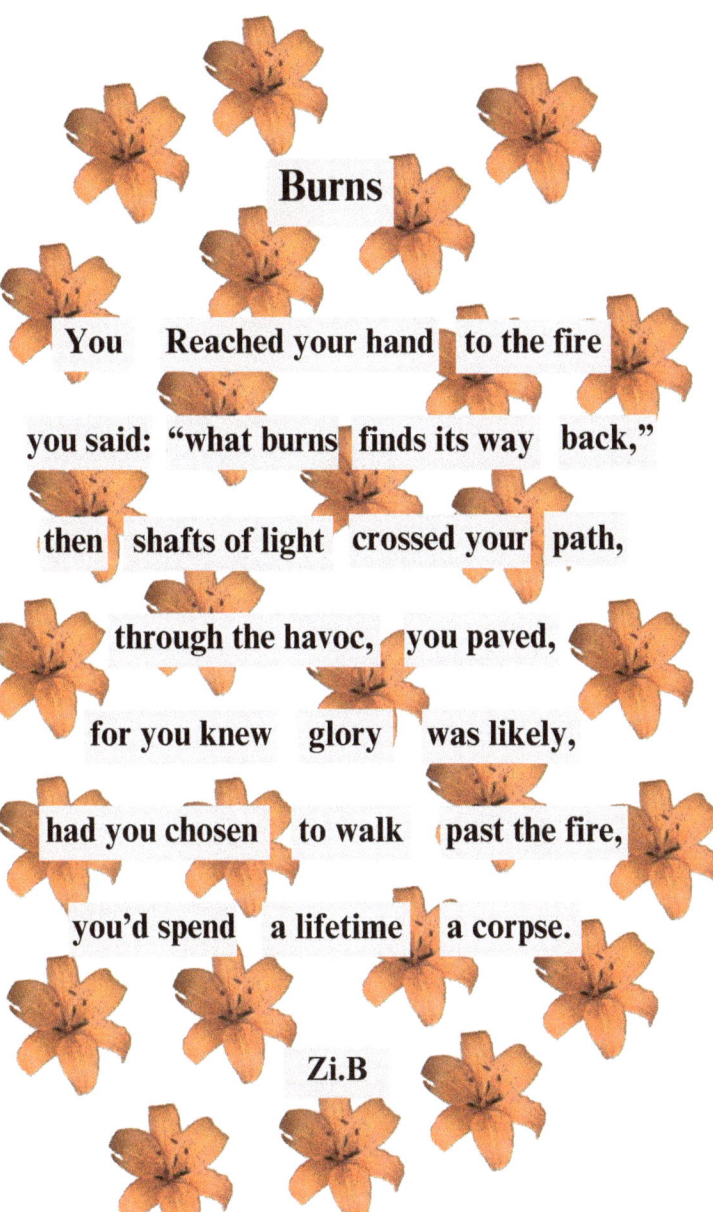

Till death DO us pART

You imperfect human

You imperfect human, I cherish you,
from my eyes, all you do is endearing,
my ears take in consideration all you say,
whether you were thoughtless or intentional.

> Your crafted persona makes you seem flawless,
> but you drip with clues of your subjective stains,
> there are places for flaws, and yours are in your head,
> they reflect kindness for you see others as you see yourself.

Zi.B

Piano notes

Define me with a string of quaint piano notes

for my song remains true to myself,

frolic to my chant

for the madness is contagious,

pirouette on the floors I built you

for the words will catch you if you fall,

dance tirelessly to this tune

for it is memorable despite its briefness.

Zi.B

My Butterfly

You have wings
butterfly
use them to leave
me
I fear I'm not able
to let go

also
tear my wings off
so I won't fly
beside you
you're meant to be
elsewhere
I don't deserve
you.

Don't look at me
with honey
dripping from your
eyes
allow me to let go

allow yourself to
expand
happiness awaits
you
in a far away land
that will never
accept me.

Zi.B

Freckle in the sky

I was adopted by the moon
became a freckle in the sky
clouds pass me by like waves
my redeemed eyes open wide
and what a view of the
ground
from above I see the truth
it prompts me to say:
"All this time we weren't in
lack,
we'd long forgotten our
purpose
and settled for fleeting bliss."

Zi.B

Motif

To be a motif on your pattern
the one you eventually
find your way back to.

What was once a fluke
is now known as fate
a déjà vu with every contact
serendipity you'll claim
when our paths reach an
intersection
and love turns you weak.

Zi.B

Never Lonely

You shall never be lonely
when your heart is connected
and your thoughts are linked
to the people you care for.

You shall never be lonely
if you trust
that there are minds alike yours
waiting
just as you are.

No distance or circumstance matters
when acknowledging feelings of care.

Protect your heart,
protect your peace,
for that is the key.

Zi.B

Paper Plane

Take me on your paper plane,
fly me out the window,
beyond our minds and this globe,
skies we pass are bleak and it makes
us sing,
our melody brings forth sourceless
nostalgia,
as though we've always been here on
this paper plane,
as though life was the dream and this
moment, reality.

The wings of your paper plane stand
strong amidst the rain,
you lift my arms back, we bask, and
soak for all thoughts pass us by,
we're consumed by feeling alone for it
isn't a thought process,
In your presence, I at last, grasp
reality,
I shall never go back,
for this paper plane solely offers a
one-way ride.

Zi.B

Lost my mind
found my soul
left me numb
to the core
white nights
brought clarity.

I won't lie
I'm not all-knowing
the more I sought
the less I knew
but I'm calmer
pleas are gone
I'm present at last.

Present by
Zi.B

Sweet

He's sweet like a wedding cake sample box
with every slice a new delight
much to choose from
but I won't choose
for I embrace them all.

His whispers tickle
they're sprinkled in the air
like cinnamon
and I melt
like the sugar cube
on his tongue.

He fermented in sugar for months
and was born a jam to no surprise
he is what he is
sweet.

Zi.B

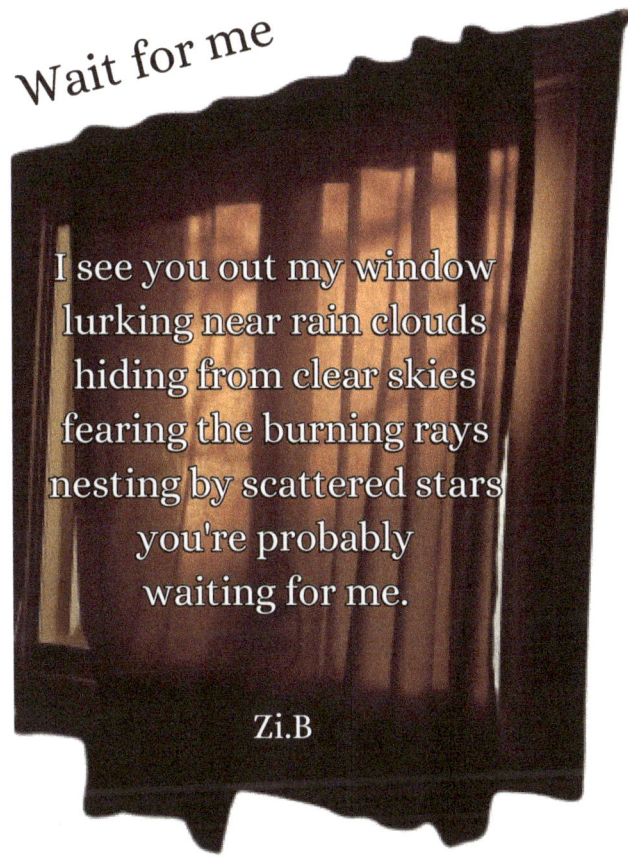

Wait for me

I see you out my window
lurking near rain clouds
hiding from clear skies
fearing the burning rays
nesting by scattered stars
you're probably
waiting for me.

Zi.B

Worth

Worth,
the word itself conveys monetary value,
I need to prove myself in order to have worth,
being alive isn't enough for them,
staying by their side seems to be a given,
I'm useless in their eyes,
worth nothing despite my unseen efforts,
I questioned it over and over for all it's worth.

Can one be worth something for the sole reason they're alive?
Is one only deserving warmth as long as they're fulfilling their duties?
Is life worth it if all you do is surviving?

For all it's worth, I simply want to be happy.

Zi.B

Love mortgage

I took a loan of eighty percent,
and gave twenty percent as a down payment,
because it was all I could afford.
When the currency is love,
I have to break the heart, not a piggy bank.
Of course, even that didn't hold much.
No regular job will reward me with love
So how can I work for love?
You don't really work for love now do you…
You receive it from someone who felt strongly about you.
You don't force love; it happens naturally.
So do I stay still and wait for it?
But they tell me to go for it, to reach out.
So I can't do anything about it, yet I should wait?
Will I ever repay my mortgage?
Will I drown in debts and have it all seized?

Zi.B

Down Blue

I'm down blue

free of all and none

Could I be bothering
all that breaths...?

I'm spiraling again

My days are blue

I wish my life were a rainbow

for not a day to pass monotonously.

I even lack the energy to go insane

can't cry or shout

It'll be fine in a few days,
as though it never happened.

Zi.B

Mystique waters

I'm suffocating in these mystique waters,
where the fish have wings yet choose to swim,
where seashell pearls are regarded as plain,
for the mystique waters favours beauty on display,
and seashells whilst not hiding, open with time.

My reflection looks at me from above the water,
my only link to the ground is extending an arm,
at times, I fear it's an illusion, a figment of my mind,
because the currents drag me so violently,
as though to say I, who strays the predetermined path
is bound to go downhill,
I stubbornly resist and go against,
for my arrow never fully reaches their side,
for I am faithful to my reflection,
which make the mystique waters seem more of an illusion than anything.

Zi.B

No free table

I understand your words
as though I've lived them
you say things I've said often
but you've never known me
we're just like-minded people
trying to uncover our purpose
find a seat at the table
that table wasn't for us though
ultimately we thought it better
to assemble our own.

Zi.B

Bask-ing

There's apricity in isolation,
lonely but bound to notice,
the quirks and the ego,
bound to bask in the rainfall,
hear the drops and feel the blues,
for the rain deserves to be loved,
and the flowers are but a destination.

Zi.B

<u>Apricity:</u> The warmth of the sun on a winter day

Purple ray

Purple is less apparent
it's faint for a full rainbow is rare
or perhaps its ray can be seen with the mind
and the mind only
it brings me to realize many are alike to it
as the entire picture is required
to see the last colour of the rainbow
so would it be for a truth
to consider every side
is the way to the purple ray.

Zi.B

Plate

You say your plate is full
well mine is hollow
void of love
void of care
overall
empty

I'm still here next to you
to yearn
I yearn for you to notice
that you take everything for
granted

your luck is running out
the link is weakening
I'm not an object
used solely when needed.

Zi.B

His angel

If he could shield her
from this world,
he would,
if it were safer in his
arms,
he'd never let go,
if she'd be willing to
renounce her wings,
he'd gladly become her
paradise,
she told him she was no
angel,
but he's not willing to
believe it,
for his mind was set at
first sight.

Zi.B

Coffee cups

table of half empty coffee cups
idle chatter ongoing
staring at the clouds
their shapes keep me lit
disappointment becomes oddly soothing
am I mistaken out of optimism
or is that all life can give me?

Zi.B

Deep Sleep

My deep sleep is untouchable,
nonsensical dreams tie my foot to the door,
hours wasted on cycling rubber bands,
unintelligible dialogue and sweet nothings,
ignored and non-present,
overlooking a world where I have no control,
much like reading the news.

My deep sleep is untouchable,
I'm a camera of many perspectives,
The camera man never dies but wishes to,
then follow the unresolved and forgotten mysteries,
My deep sleep matters little, yet affects greatly.

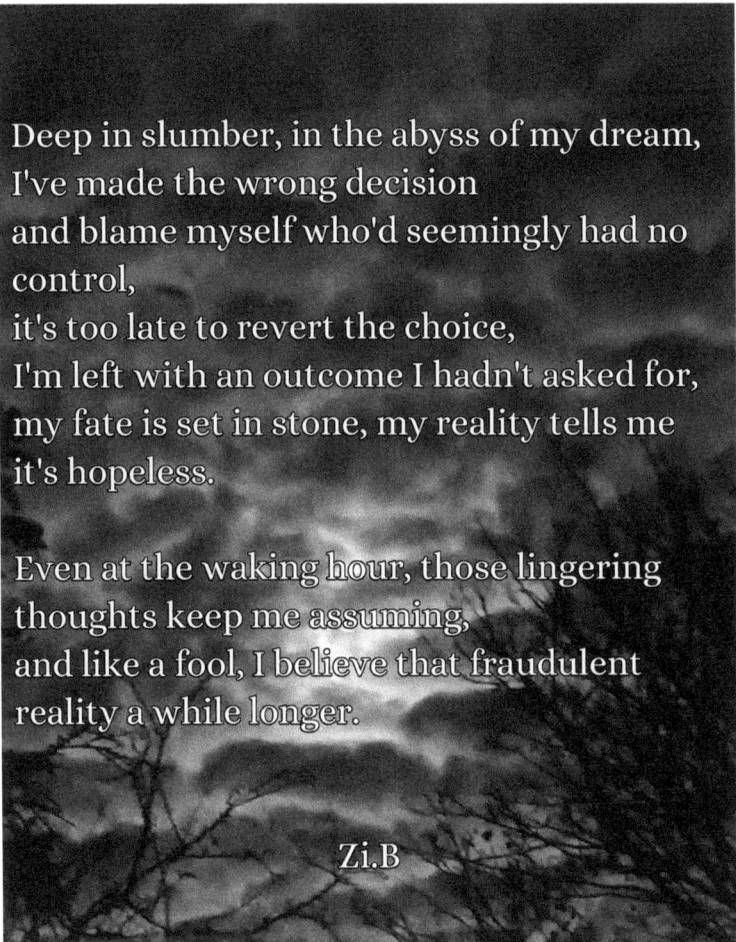

Deep in slumber, in the abyss of my dream,
I've made the wrong decision
and blame myself who'd seemingly had no control,
it's too late to revert the choice,
I'm left with an outcome I hadn't asked for,
my fate is set in stone, my reality tells me it's hopeless.

Even at the waking hour, those lingering thoughts keep me assuming,
and like a fool, I believe that fraudulent reality a while longer.

Zi.B

Rain song

Rain is our theme song,
when it pours I raise my gaze to clouds,
for I might find you there,
singing along with an angelic voice,
till one reaches out with compassion,
or at the very least, awareness.

At times you think it's all in vain,
let me remind you
that my thoughts wander your way,
for every day I live,
and likewise, it keeps me going.

Let me be the one,
to tell you rain is falling,
not you,
you're standing in the midst,
for you've only inherited rain's charm,
not its sorrows.

Won't you tell me
I'm not alone
when I think of you
in the rain.

Zi.B

Dream child

My dream is my child
I cherish it as so
for my child is bright
and the source of my joy.

While our world is complex,
and arduous to strive in
I have faith in my child
as its greatest believer.

My dream
which is my child
shall be treated
with respect
and trust.

I support my creation
like a parent
expecting nothing
but the happiness
of their children.

Zi.B

My very own traitor

I cling to the memory of a past dream
with a poem I had written then
for my brain betrays me with ease.

A traitor adhering to darkness
as though it were second nature
then abandons the light
for it proved to be laborious
contrary to the effortless road
of negativity.

I persist without logic
for that wouldn't matter
in a combat free of rationality.

Perhaps I'll invent facts
and they'll become truth.

Zi.B

An apple fell on my head

I fell for you like Newton's apple,
I too discovered gravity that day,
I realized you'd be the only to hold me down,
the constant pull of your gaze keeps me afloat,
I cannot escape you, it's a law of physics.

Zi.B

Better than stars

Extending an arm to the sky,
I'm able to meet stars,
hold a few of them,
how dear they are.

I yearn to be held like stars

Contrary to stars, I'm near,
not blinding to the eyes,
or hot to the touch,

Will I ever be
better than stars
for you?

Zi.B

The Tide

Sea water drips down my eyes,
See the pain I carried in the depths,
It's boldly uncovered by the crashing waves,
The mist wears it like gold chains,
Breath my air, revere to it,
I'm still here, shot but not down.

Zi.B

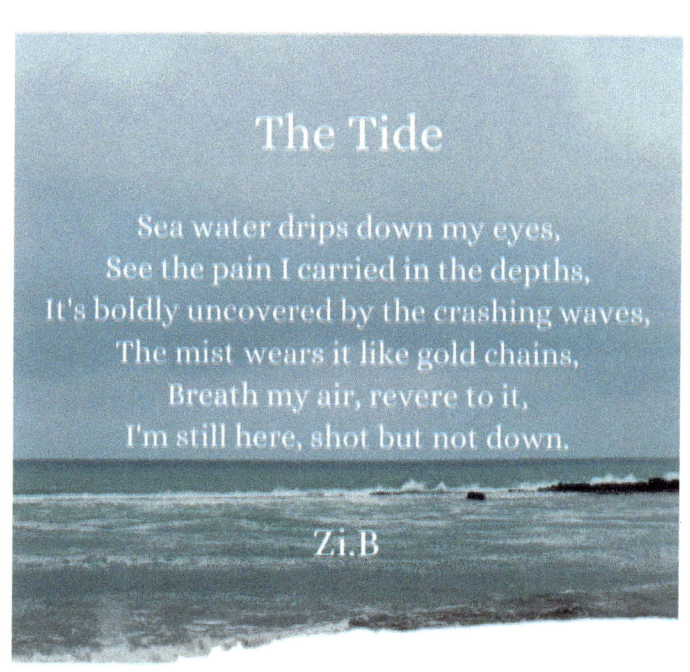

The Tide

Sea water drips down my eyes,
See the pain I carried in the depths,
It's boldly uncovered by the crashing waves,
The mist wears it like gold chains,
Breath my air, revere to it,
I'm still here, shot but not down.

Zi.B

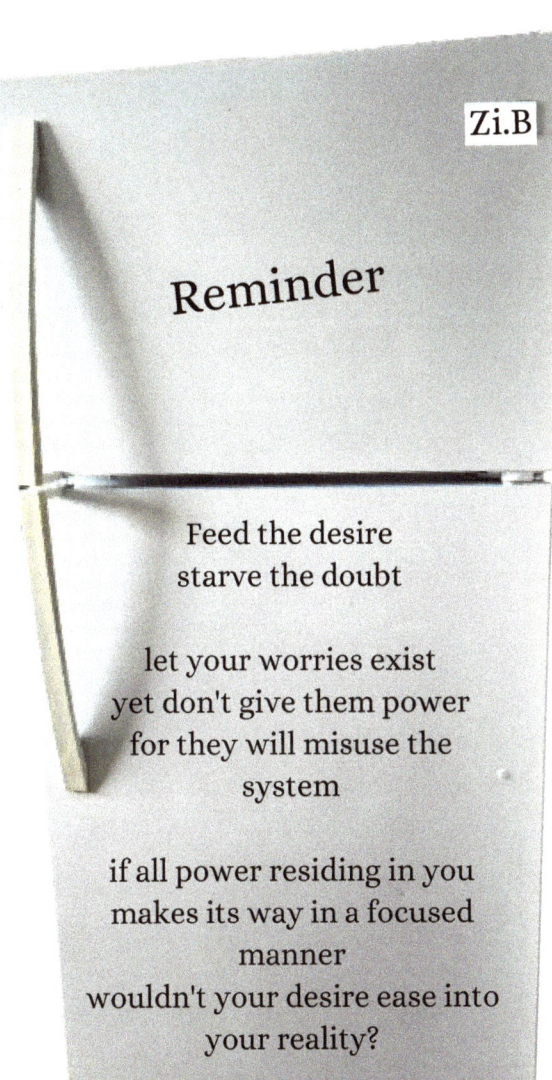

Zi.B

Reminder

Feed the desire
starve the doubt

let your worries exist
yet don't give them power
for they will misuse the system

if all power residing in you
makes its way in a focused manner
wouldn't your desire ease into your reality?

Common sense

Common sense is lost,
It's not worth speaking anymore,
aware that silence is also cause for criticism,
I am afraid,
afraid to be ripped apart for absurd
entertainment,
The main character of the week's gossip.

Common sense is lost again,
It's spiraling away
to a land I wished were home.

My hope goes to the ones
whose modern minds aren't tarnished
by the multitude of senseless opinions,
for I'm lonely in this avalanche
of self-proclaimed righteous people.

Zi.B

In the stars

I've faced you before
at night
in the stars
hidden in plain sight
you're easily seen by the naked eye
I'll ask you again and again
do you come from my paradise
the one I face on certain nights
because I've dreamt of you
as many times as I can count sheep
I think it's kismet
that we live in the same universe
and it's poetry that brings me to you
the blur fades and here we are
scattered amongst every matter
sailing with our madness
expanding the universe
here we are
in the stars

Zi.B

The moon rests a kiss atop my head,
There's a long night ahead of me,
Raindrops free fall to their own puddles,
I extend my umbrella to the sky's murmurs,
To the rhythm of my humming, I pitter patter,
That mist is here to stay, it waits for none.

The night wraps around me like a cloak,
It keeps me mellow, promises me a rainbow,
My night seldom ends with the rising of the sun
My night eerily hums in reminder of the war in my mind.

Zi.B

Hum

Dancing in the dark

We're dancing in the dark
eyes closed for there is no use
hand in hand fingertips brushing
incontrollable bubbling in my stomach
I'm drowning in the ballroom
our dance shall never end
for it plays in my head unrelentingly
like figurines in a music box.

Zi.B

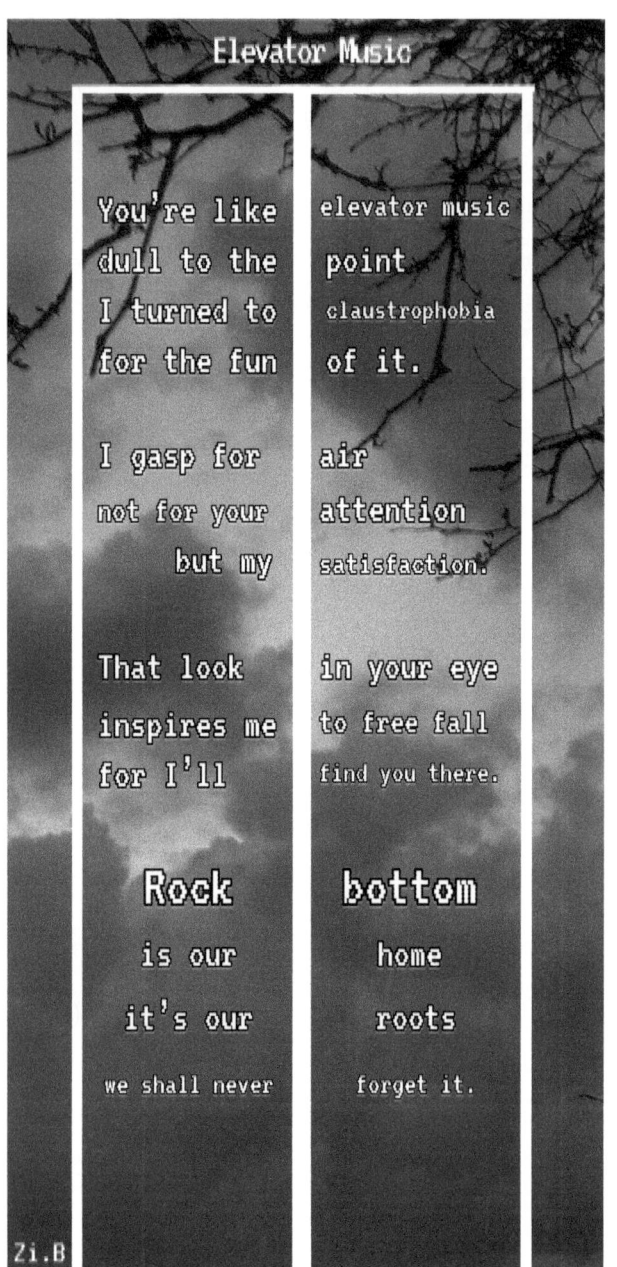

Elevator Music

You're like elevator music
dull to the point
I turned to claustrophobia
for the fun of it.

I gasp for air
not for your attention
but my satisfaction.

That look in your eye
inspires me to free fall
for I'll find you there.

Rock **bottom**
is our home
it's our roots
we shall never forget it.

Zi.B

Groundless

I was made for the ground rather than currents,
no matter how blind you are to the flow,
you must realize it isn't by choice you are following,
you are not swimming if the water moves you.

You mustn't think yourself better,
even when your waters are stable
and my ground is shaking,
you mustn't criticize me later,
when flowers grow on my ground
and you are drowning in your stable waters.

The mirror I hold might scare you,
or at least plunge you into reflection,
but don't be frightened for tomorrow
can be unlike any day you've known,
if you can put a foot on your ground.

Zi.B

Pictograms

Photographs scattered on the table
each so foreign I question my past
the fog in my head is ever so subtle
whilst the rain alongside it is lethal.

Memories are tangled
to the point of illegibility
pictograms without labels
mismatched boxes of clutter
echoes growing in the distance
escaping with exiting signals.

Zi.B

Mind like a universe

Iridescence from your eyes
you see through veil and body
all in contrasting lights
for you consider more than provided
and open your mind
to endless possibilities.

In your eyes I'll forever remain a mystery
like the constantly expanding universe
you don't mind leaving questions pending
you honour my ever changing mind
I couldn't ask for more than this
and I vow to mirror your intentions
given that I too respect your mind.

Zi.B

Is anybody out there?

You just want to feel something again
the tears don't crawl out anymore
you don't seek help because you know
you know none will reach out
you've been there plenty of times
and never out.

Words in your head flow without purpose
"Does anything really matter
why is everybody so serious
when life is so..."

Hatred takes over for there is no love
frustration till it becomes despair

Is there a way out?
Is it worth looking for?
Who knows what's out there...

All that I can tell you
is I'm just like you
can't that be enough
to be aware you're not alone in this world.

Zi.B

Mind reader

You're no mind reader, never will be
It's mocking to claim you know me,
Question me but don't answer yourself,
For you'll most likely be mistaken,
You'll be left disillusioned,
For I'm not up to par,
Unless you wanted to think less of me,
To be proved right,
In your world only,
Because who am I to interfere there?

Zi.B

Mortal lover

You've loved many before me,

Although they've left you with scars,

Can I kiss them away?

Can I be your world?

Can the past be irrelevant,

and the future ours as is the present?

I don't want to feel green,

I don't want to show insecurities,

Your experience scares me,

You're my first and I'm one of for you,

There's nothing wrong with that,

It's just I wish I was your first,

But I know I'm the one who lasted,

The one whose mind goes right in yours,

I'm your mortal lover.

Zi.B

Lost souls

We're lost souls drawn to lies
content with our structure
I assume
for the saying 'life's unfair'
was man made.

We berate pain
yet compete
for the title of
most pained.

we measure pain
but disregard variables
for even logic
is subjective at times.

Zi.B

The trilogy of you

I.
My hand in yours, I'm soothed,
your grip is so firm, fear concedes,
then your eyebrows arch with empathy,
I've never seen kinder eyes,
I had thought of your kindness as a weakness,
in time I understood it was your essence,
a requisite to your character.

Zi.B

The trilogy of you

II.

I want to wear you like a wedding band,
weld you around my finger like a promise
for I've never encountered such magnetism
for my thoughts have found their muse
and for the doubts have never lacked this much authority.

Zi.B

The trilogy of you

III. My head is saturated with words you spoke
in that voice laced with eternal sunshine
were it in my power
I'd have your sound narrate my every thought.

Zi.B

The other side

like a mirror I see myself in you
and like my reflection
I can reach a hand
knowing it won't reach the other side

trapped in my respective world
I see you daily
yet still wait for you mostly
would it be over
if the mirror shattered in petty shards
would our words collide
or would they loose contact...

Zi.B

Kooky cookie

played hooky for a cookie
a freaky cookie nearly fancy
dipped in whisky
plunged in honey
crazy cookie you could say
nearly sloppy barely pretty
little heavy maybe worthy
hands are sticky slowly dirty
hooked on a cookie early copy

Zi.B

Bring me back to the sea

Bring me back to the sea
I promise I won't leave this time
things matter less and I'm able to be selfish
let me witness the sun's sleep patterns
in the comfort of the sea whose tide is wild
and whose waves sing a never ending recital
bring me back to the sand who burns only for a while
I promise I won't curse at it no matter the pain
I'll keep an eye on the water, make sure it never empties
it's already been occupying my mind from afar
things won't change following the wish fulfilled
for I am a lover all the same
so till my end let me be where I feel most alive
where my love is easier done, than said.

Zi.B

Summer

I long for summer
every day it isn't summer,
I crave the heat when the cold burns,
clothes are warm but too heavy
I miss skin exposure,
I crave the sun's kisses
like a lover misses its soulmate
across the globe,
I thought summer was a place
but a place doesn't leave
a person does,
summer is equal to a lover,
summer is a person I love.

Zi.B

Winterfall Ablaze

Winter is failing
winter is falling
I run across
with glory and fire
melting it all
from snowflakes
to negatives in the air
It's all tainted now
in multi colour
on paper and ground
Winterfall is ablaze
and I am blooming
a lavender at a time.

Zi.B

Pages of notes

*lines that didn't make the cut
(poems I could never finish)*

Zi.B

My memory is blurry
not because it is fading
but because I've captured it that way
my perception of that situation
was wrong.

                                      I've been cleansed by the sun
                                             rid of my shadow
                                               the glamour is off
                                         we're ready to talk now

4am was a blur
a circle of doubts
feeding me lies
poisoning my mind
creating weakness
making me lose strength
till conviction was lost

Do I understand you
or do I assume I do
because we're so similar?

> Twenty four hours passed,
> here I am, wide awake,
> no awful thoughts dash,
> the mood is stable,
> perhaps I'm a little too calm,
> I sit at my desk and remember
> that every moment has its end,

Don't pull me in the water,
water's heavy and
your pressure is suffocating.

I don't care, I don't care, someone tell me I'm doing the right thing. Someone counter their words. Someone...

My eyes may not be blue but I can choose to see it all in blue,
the layer I cannot see without a mirror matters little,
for my mind changes like a chameleon

I feel I do not perceive the world with eyes but with mind,
it starts with a thought before it is reflected by that avenue,
the contrary now seems to be an illusion

I've gone mad for the seventh time today,

-

I take delight in the torture my mind puts me through,

-

The core of my madness is _____
At the core of my madness we find _____

Self awareness was necessary,
Without it we're puppets,
I can't connect with people attached to the strings,
I thought I envied them because it was so painful to be aware,
Now not a gram of me envies the unaware,

Simplicity was all we needed all along,
Us, the overthinkers,
The ones crafting mind problems in mere seconds,

It's not the end of the world,
but it could lead to it,
to its demise, its downfall.

I smell your perfume out of the blue,
At least that's how I imagine you'd smell like

There were many lines before a much simpler one,
Full sentences written to be erased for I could not
find the right words.
I still typed the words I knew weren't perfect,
thinking it'd bring me closer to the desired

What am I if not insane?
Have I ever been sane?
This pain I'll gladly bear,
It's nothing to fear,
So what if I'm a bit insane, aren't we all?
The normal we wear as a nametag is a decoy,

She writes what she cannot live,
unaware her thoughts are foreshadowing.
She escapes to worlds unbelievable to her mind,

How old do you think I look?
Too young to drink a double long espresso,
Too old to be rotting in my room without contact,
Am I mature when I speak but immature by the way
I live?

There's an inadequate sphere hanging in the sky,
some call it a satellite, while others their mother,
some believe it to be their safety pin, while some feel it cries of loneliness,
such a mysterious presence

Everyone needs a fantasy,
a place to escape with the mind,
it's a power unique to us,
neglected by many who feel it worthless,
it costs nothing to dream,
you won't lose what you've never owned,

Dream sellers opened shop in a desolate place
where dreamers wail in despair

I've always wondered why they sold dreams
when they could live theirs

brought me out of my shell,
shadows of water propagate
freckles of the sky look over us
curiosity of a city under sea

There's a city under wraps,
under layers of water,

gently drowning in your depths

Memories created in my mind
at times, feel more real than physically lived memories

Thank you

Thank you for reading the first edition of Notes & Camera roll. I am eternally grateful you even picked this book. The process of creating this book will forever be one I remember. Despite it not being my first book, that feeling somehow is there. It is the first of a new series. I also believe the books I published prior made me discover the fact that I was meant to do more. It all led to 'Notes & Camera Roll'. Therefore, I genuinely feel like my career is just beginning.

Whether you are reading this before the release of other editions or much later along the journey, I once again want to thank you for being part of it. If you came here to feel something, I hope you did. If knowing someone else felt the same as you brings you to feel less lonely, then one of my missions is accomplished. Would it be bold of me to tell you: "You aren't alone?" The audacity to say that without backing the claim, you might think. I understand. I feel the same. So let us navigate through understanding why we are not alone together.

cannot wait to thank you again at the end of the next edition. Believe or not, that book is already a work in progress. I cannot stop writing poetry. It's in my nature as much as it keeps me alive.

Playlist

I'd love to recommend you some songs I've been listening to while working on this book. Music is the next best thing in my life after writing; therefore, I found it fitting to share here.

DPR IAN - His entire discography

However my favourite song is Winterfall :)

Lana Del Rey - Terrence loves you

but also her entire discography and everybody else's on this list! I do have to recommend specific songs...

Reed Wonder & Aurora Olivas - Alive Again

Lolo Zouaï - Chevy Impala

Mac Ayres - Alone with you

PLAZA - Voodoo II

Jenevieve - Love Quotes

Naïka - On My Way

Again, all of these artist's discographies are immaculate and it was incredibly difficult to choose a song.

Submissions

If you have a poem you'd like to share with the world and or a yearning to make yourself known as a poet, perhaps you'd like to submit a poem.

I do want this book series to be a method of communication, as it takes two to tango, it also takes at least two to communicate. Please do share with me your poem, your thoughts, and perhaps see it in the next edition? I do not judge a poem objectively because I believe the art of it is subjective. Don't be afraid and take a chance.

I hope to be able to display a few poems written by others in my next book. Fingers crossed!

Of course, if you do not have a poem to share but simply thoughts, please do so; I'd love to hear anything you have to say.

Submit on "zinebbizriken.space"

- There is no minimum or maximum word count
- if you have a book to promote and or a social media platform, leave me the details
- Please submit only one poem

Try writing a poem?
It can be therapeutic

www.ingramcontent.com/pod-product-compliance
Lightning Source LLC
Chambersburg PA
CBHW061740070526
44585CB00024B/2754